AUTUMN FESTIVALS

Mike Rosen

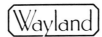

Seasonal Festivals

Autumn Festivals
Winter Festivals
Spring Festivals
Summer Festivals

Editors: Tracey Smith and Geraldine Purcell
Designer: Ross George

Cover: Child at Hallowe'en, Northern Ireland

First published in 1990 by
Wayland (Publishers) Limited
61 Western Road, Hove
East Sussex, BN3 1JD, England

British Library Cataloguing in Publication Data
Rosen, Mike 1959–
   Autumn festivals.
   1. Festivals
   I. Title II. Series
   394.2

   ISBN 1–85210–878–9

Typeset by Rachel Gibbs, Wayland
Printed by G. Canale C.S.p.A., Turin
Bound by Casterman S.A., Belgium.

Contents

Autumn

As the heat of summer fades, autumn begins. Each evening the sun sets a little earlier; each morning it rises a little later. In the temperate parts of the world, between the tropics and the polar regions, many trees shed their leaves for winter. Before they fall the leaves change colour. Some leaves turn quickly from deep green to bright yellow and others go through shades of russet, red and orange. In the golden sunlight of an autumn evening, whole forests seem to light up in a mass of glowing colours.

Below During autumn, the leaves of many trees change colour before dropping from the branches in the winter. This picture shows this beautiful colour change.

Most mornings in late autumn are so cold that the grass and fallen leaves are stiff with frost, their frozen surfaces glittering as if covered in tiny jewels. Those animals which hibernate prepare for their winter sleep; others search for food to put in their winter stores. People also prepare for winter; they may finish repairs to their houses, check their heating systems or build up stocks of firewood. For farmers, autumn is the time for late harvests and ploughing, or moving animals from the summer pastures into shelter. It is a time for festivals which celebrate another fruitful year's farming.

Above **These sheaves of wheat have been bound together in a traditional style. They are standing in a field, ready to be collected.**

Food Festivals

For thousands of years people have grown food. The earliest crops included cereal grasses and grains. The early farmers did their best to look after the crops, but often disease or bad weather ruined them before they were ready for harvest. People knew that when their crops failed, they would face severe hunger and maybe even death. A good harvest was a time for celebration.

Today farming is more efficient in most parts of the world. Fertilizers help many farmers to grow two harvests each year. Vegetables are often grown in enormous greenhouses, which are run like factories. These buildings can be

Below **These Amish farmers in the USA prefer to use traditional methods rather than machinery to gather their crops. It is long and tiring work and many people are needed to bring the harvest safely home.**

used to produce food all year round, despite bad weather. Most countries have stores of food in warehouses which they can use if the year's harvest fails. Food grown in one country can be transported quickly to any part of the world that needs it. Farming has changed much over the centuries, but the harvest is still celebrated in a traditional way by many people.

Many major religious events take some of their character from older harvest festivals. Apart from those celebrated by Christians, there are Jewish festivals such as Shavuot and Succoth, and the Sikh festival Baisakhi. In African countries where there are large numbers of Christians, harvest festivals often take place in autumn, but they are celebrated with rituals which date from long before Christianity was brought to Africa.

Above **Most fruit is too delicate to be picked by machine. Fruit picking provides work in autumn for many people all over the world.**

7

Some Harvest Festivals

In the world's temperate zones the harvest season starts in the spring and ends in late autumn. One of the first harvests each year is winter barley. Then there are crops of fruit and vegetables before the wheat and grain are ready in summer. As autumn arrives, in the temperate zones there are late fruits such as apples to collect, and in many Asian countries, rice harvests.

There is almost always a celebration of some sort after a harvest is complete, when workers enjoy themselves with a feast and a party. This celebration may include singing and dancing. It may be a small party, just for the people from one farm, or it may be a feast for all the workers in an area.

Above **This picture shows rice harvesting in Bali. Some tropical Asian countries are able to collect two rice harvests each year.**

8

Many countries also have one major festival to celebrate the whole year's harvests. Christians attend special services, taking with them fruits and vegetables from their gardens or something they have made. There may also be corn dollies. These are made from the last stalks of corn to be cut and, traditionally, are ploughed into the soil before the seed is sown for next year's crop. In Britain there are several special harvest festivals. Some are held by the market traders of London, who parade in fantastic suits, covered with pearl buttons. These people are called Pearly Kings and Queens. Harvest festivals are also popular among fishermen in Britain. These celebrate a good season's fishing.

There are autumn festivals linked to old harvest traditions, which are held for other reasons. One example is the Bavarian Oktoberfest. First held in 1723 to celebrate the king's marriage, it has become an annual event, filled with feasting and drinking.

Left **This Pearly King and Queen are wearing traditional costumes. Their custom of decorating coats and trousers with pearl buttons began in nineteenth-century London.**

Thanksgiving Days

When the first Europeans settled in America they arrived too late to sow crops for the following year's harvest. Nearly half the settlers died of starvation during that first winter. The next spring, those who had survived were able to plant their seeds and, after an excellent summer harvest, they celebrated with a festival. The festival became known as Thanksgiving Day, and in 1941 it was given the fixed date each year of the fourth Thursday in November.

Food is an important part of Thanksgiving celebrations. Traditional thanksgiving foods include turkey, which is eaten with cranberry

Below **At Thanksgiving Americans and Canadians like to celebrate with a big family meal. They traditionally eat such foods as turkey and cranberry sauce.**

sauce, and pumpkin pie. At Thanksgiving, as many of the family as possible will gather together. Like many other public holidays, Thanksgiving is often celebrated with street parties and sporting events.

Thanksgiving is also celebrated in Canada, where it is held on the second Monday in October. Canadians hold Thanksgiving before the Americans because winter begins earlier in Canada than the USA.

In Japan, one of the most important harvests is that of the autumn rice crop. Traditionally, none of the newly-grown rice could be eaten until a ceremony had been held to honour the spirits which were thought to protect the rice while it grew. There was a procession and a great banquet, at which ceremonial dances were performed. At midnight, the Emperor of Japan took part in a ritual, presenting a portion of the harvest at a sacred altar. Today the festival is a public holiday, when people celebrate the success of Japanese industry and farming. It is called Labour Thanksgiving Day.

Above **At the end of the rice harvest in Japan there is a national festival to celebrate the success of all Japanese workers.**

Tropical Harvest Festivals

In some tropical areas there can be harvests all year round of different fruit and vegetables. Elsewhere in the tropics a successful harvest may depend on the right weather conditions, in the same way as in the temperate zones. Most countries in South East Asia have three seasons – one dry, one rainy, and one cold. The rainy season starts in some countries during July and finishes towards the end of October. However, most countries do not have rain for such a long time.

In the state of Kerala, on the southern tip of India, there is a harvest festival called Onam at the end of the rainy season. People clean their houses thoroughly and decorate the floors. Children collect flowers such as poppies, lilies, and marigolds from the fields and roadsides. These flowers are then woven into colourful mats. In return for their work,

Above **Farmers in Kerala use much traditional machinery. The plough this farmer is using is pulled by oxen. Cattle are regarded as holy animals for many Indians.**

the children receive new clothes.

Once the preparations are complete, people visit the temple to give thanks for the harvest. Then there is a magnificent feast of rice, vegetables and spiced curries, followed by sweet puddings. After this, boat races are held on the lagoons along the shore. The boats are long and sleek with intricate carvings on the prow or stern. Popular designs include snakes' heads and birds' tails.

There are many different sorts of harvest festival in Africa. Some African countries have a Christian celebration in autumn. Others celebrate in the traditional African style with music and dance. The dancers wear masks and dance with steps and patterns that each have a meaning. They tell a story and try to frighten or honour the spirits which they believe affect a good harvest.

Below **The music of the talking drum (shown here) is an important part of many West African festivals. Music and dancing often form an important part of festival celebrations.**

New Year Festivals

One of the most important days in autumn is the equinox. At this time, the hours of daylight equal the hours of darkness. After the equinox, the days become shorter than the nights. Early in their history, humans realized the importance of the sun to life on earth. In the period after the autumn equinox the sun appears to be weakening in its struggle against darkness. To help the sun regain its strength ancient peoples held festivals of light with torchlit processions and blazing bonfires.

Some autumn festivals which celebrate historical events use lights and fires. The Jewish festival Chanukah, in early December, remembers when the Jews recaptured their temple in Jerusalem over 2,000 years ago. One of the rituals of Chanukah involves lighting

Below **Chanukah celebrations in an Israeli synagogue. The six lighted candles show it is the sixth evening of Chanukah.**

candles each evening – one candle for each day of the festival. By the last evening of Chanukah eight candles are burning together.

The autumn equinox has been used to mark the start of a new year by many societies. The ancient Celtic tribes of northern Europe held a New Year festival at the end of October, with bonfires and feasting. Other autumn New Year festivals are the Jewish celebration Rosh Hashanah and, for some Hindus, the festival of Diwali.

In the tropics the length of day varies little throughout the year, and the autumn equinox seems less important. Because of this, most autumn equinox festivals come from areas further away from the Equator – Europe, Central Asia, Northern India, China, and the southern parts of South America.

Above **The candleholder used in the Chanukah celebrations is called a menorah. All eight candles have now been lit.**

Bonfire Night

Guy Fawkes Night, or Bonfire Night, is celebrated in Britain on the 5 November. Around this time, streets and playing fields echo to the explosions of fireworks. Many people go to firework displays. Everyone tries to get a good view of the fireworks and children wave sparklers, making dancing patterns of light in the smoky dusk.

Excitement grows as the fireworks begin. Huge rockets shoot into the sky, exploding with a blaze of coloured stars and ear-splitting noise. Catherine wheels spin madly in a circle of sparks while other fireworks shoot fountains of coloured flames many metres off the ground. After the fireworks, a huge bonfire is lit. A figure made from straw or paper

Left In the days leading up to Bonfire Night children often make a model of Guy Fawkes from straw and old clothes. This is set up in the street and the children then ask for 'a penny for the guy'. This photograph was taken in France, where these children have adopted the British tradition of making such a guy.

stuffed into old clothes is put on the top of the fire and, when it begins to burn, the crowd cheers. This figure, or guy, represents Guy Fawkes, who was accused of trying to blow up the British Houses of Parliament in November 1605 and was later executed.

Autumn bonfire festivals were held long before Guy Fawkes. The ancient Celtic peoples of Britain celebrated their New Year with bonfires and feasts at the start of November. These traditions were continued in many parts of Britain long after the Christian Church became powerful. When people looked for a way to celebrate the failure of Guy Fawkes' plot, they used the customs of their traditional November bonfire festival. In this way, an ancient seasonal festival was given new life by historical events.

Above **Bonfires were built during November as part of the ancient Celtic festival of Samhain many centuries before they were linked with Guy Fawkes Night celebrations.**

Diwali

Left This colourful poster advertises the festival of Diwali. The celebration of this festival is often very exciting, with brightly coloured lights decorating homes and public buildings.

Diwali is a Festival of Lights, celebrated by both Hindus and Sikhs. For some Hindus it traditionally marks the start of a new financial or farming year; Sikhs remember the release from prison of Guru Hargobind, who was the sixth Sikh Guru. Although these two religions keep Diwali for different reasons, the festival is celebrated in a similar way by both Hindus and Sikhs.

The lights of Diwali are one of India's most spectacular sights. The festival is held at the new moon in late October or early November, when the nights are long and very dark. In villages, towns and cities the darkness is pierced by the light from small lamps or candles, placed in the doorways and windows of houses. Many of the lights are traditional pottery oil lamps, known as divas, which give off a warm golden light. In the evenings there are dramatic firework displays which fill the sky with noise and blazing colours.

Since Diwali is, for some Hindus, a New Year festival, many celebrate with rituals to honour Lakshmi, their goddess of prosperity. So that Lakshmi will help the family in the new year the house is cleaned and new or specially washed clothes are worn. Hindus believe that if they or their houses are dirty on Diwali night then Lakshmi will not want to visit them. In parts of northern India, young girls place divas on small rafts, leaving them to float down a river. If the lamp stays alight until it has floated out of sight its owner will have good fortune that year.

Below **A central part of the Diwali celebration for Hindus in many parts of the world is the retelling of the Rama and Sita story. This celebrates the return of Rama and Sita to the village of Ayodhya as told in the Ramayana. The Lights of Diwali represent the candles that were lit to guide Rama and Sita safely home.**

Moon Festivals

Left These children are getting ready to celebrate the Chinese Festival of the Autumn Moon.

Since early human societies, calendars have been organized around the waxing and waning of the moon. Many religious festivals happen at new or full moons. These include Easter, Diwali, most Islamic holy days, many Chinese celebrations and Buddhist festivals such as Kathina.

After the autumn equinox, when the sun's power appears to decline and the nights grow longer, the moon seems to gain in the struggle against darkness. Many major moon festivals happen in autumn. One of these is celebrated in China during September, at full moon in the eighth month of the Chinese lunar calendar. On that evening a feast is held with traditional foods, such as crab meat followed by fruits and little rice cakes shaped like a full moon. These rice cakes once played an important part in Chinese history. When the Chinese successfully rebelled against their Mongol rulers in the fourteenth century, the messages giving the time and place of the rebellion were hidden in rice cakes.

Before the feast there is a procession when everybody carries a lantern shaped like an animal, bird or fish. Inside each lantern is a candle because, like other autumn festivals, the Moon Festival is celebrated partly as a Festival of Lights. Since the Chinese call the moon the Queen of Heaven this is also a festival for women, when they ask the moon for good fortune in the months which follow.

Left **Many festivals have certain foods which are linked with their celebration. Moon cakes are a traditional food at the Chinese Festival of the Autumn Moon.**

21

Dassehra and Durga Puja

Dassehra and Durga Puja are held over ten days between the first new moon and full moon after the autumn equinox. Both festivals may celebrate the Ramayana, which tells the story of Rama. In the Ramayana the demon Ravana kidnaps Sita, wife of Prince Rama. After many bloody battles, Rama eventually defeats Ravana, rescues Sita and the couple return to their home village.

At Dassehra the story of the Ramayana is told in a play, the Ram Lila, the performance of which may be spread over ten evenings. On the final night, the climax of the struggle is depicted in the most spectacular moment of the festival. Straw figures of the demon Ravana and his allies, 25 m tall, are set alight

Left These two actors are wearing the dazzling costumes used in performances of the Ramayana. Many hours of hard work go into this celebration.

with flaming arrows. Inside the figures are fireworks and, as the straw begins to burn, these explode amid great cheers from the audience.

Although the details of the Ramayana are complicated, its tale of a contest between Good and Evil may reflect the state of the sun and moon at the first new moon after the autumn equinox. Darkness seems to have stolen the moon from a weakening sun, but the Ramayana may remind its listeners that the sun will eventually regain its strength and the moon will return.

Durga Puja honours Durga, the goddess who helped Rama. The festival is celebrated with parades, dances, and performances of the Ram Lila. In the temples people give presents of flowers, rice or grain to the goddess. On the tenth day, images of Durga are taken down to the sea or a river and set afloat to drift until they finally sink into the water.

Above **At Durga Puja magnificent models such as these are paraded through the streets before being set afloat on the river.**

Festivals of Remembrance

Left At Hallowe'en people often hold fancy-dress parties. Lanterns are made by fixing candles in large hollowed-out vegetables such as pumpkins. These lamps may be made to look frightening by having a face carved in them, through which the light of the candle can shine.

The ancient Celtic peoples of north-west Europe celebrated New Year between the autumn equinox and the winter solstice – around the start of November. At the same time they honoured the spirits of their dead family and friends with a feast and bonfires. As Christianity spread in the Celtic lands during the ninth century, the Celtic festival was used as a base for a new Christian holy day. To the Christians the spirits the Celts had worshipped were evil and, as a defence against pagan evil, 1 November was made All Saints'

Day, or All Hallows. One hundred and fifty years later, the Christian Church chose 2 November as All Souls' Day. On All Souls' Day Christians remember those who have died and pray that their souls may enter Heaven.

Despite the Christian Church's efforts, Celtic traditions continued in a festival that became known as Hallowe'en. This is held on 31 October, the evening of All Hallows. At Hallowe'en parties, people often dress as witches and ghosts, or wear frightening masks. A Hallowe'en lantern consists of a large hollowed-out vegetable, such as a pumpkin, with a candle fixed inside it. In the USA at Hallowe'en, children play tricks on adults who refuse to give them a treat when they knock on their door. This is similar to the Celtic belief that spirits would use their powers against anyone who failed to honour them at the New Year festival.

Japanese Buddhists also honour their dead at the autumn equinox Higan ceremony. This is a serious occasion, when Buddhists visit the memorials to their friends and relations, to clean them and repair any damage.

Festival of Kali

Left **This poster shows the figure of the goddess Kali. This frightening goddess is seen here waving a bloodstained sword.**

While much of India is celebrating Diwali the people of Bengal are holding a festival in honour of Kali, the goddess of strength, disease and death. Followers of Kali believe that to enjoy life it is necessary to accept death as part of being human.

During the Festival of Kali, homes are strung with lights, and the streets are lined with shrines. The shrines are of many sizes, depending on the wealth of the family or group

which builds it, but they are all similar in design. Each is hung with a backdrop of cloth in brilliant colours. The edges of the shrine are decorated with flowers and incense burners; in the centre of each shrine is an image of Kali. She is shown with a fierce expression, wearing a necklace made of skulls, and with her arms uplifted. As evening comes, each shrine is lit by the yellow light of oil lamps. The streets are alive with the flickering lights that illuminate the many shrines.

Worshippers walk the streets throughout the day and evening of the festival, meeting friends and stopping at shrines to offer gifts in honour of Kali. Delicious foods are sold by street-traders and the smell of cooking fills the air. As night falls there are exciting and colourful firework displays. Finally, all the images of Kali are taken from the shrines and, in a noisy procession, they are carried down to a river. The crowds sing, chant and ring bells as each of the images of Kali is set afloat on the water. With this ceremony, the Festival of Kali ends for another year.

Jewish New Year

Rosh Hashanah and Yom Kippur are the most important times during the Ten Days of Repentance. This period in the Jewish calendar combines the main elements of most autumn celebrations. It is the Jewish New Year, and a festival of lights, but also a time for remembering the dead. The Ten Days of Repentance begin at the first new moon after the autumn equinox. This may fall in either late September or early October.

The festival begins with the two days of Rosh Hashanah. Many Jews go to the synagogue in the morning and evening of both days. After the evening service there are celebration meals at which families, workers, or members of a synagogue may eat together.

Left **This musical instrument is called a shofar. It is made from a ram's horn and is blown at both Rosh Hashanah and Yom Kippur.**

Part of this meal will be a sweet bread called challah, which is dipped in honey to remind people of the good things which the new year may bring.

During the days after Rosh Hashanah, Jews think about their actions and thoughts during the past year. If they feel they have done wrong, they will ask the victim of their actions to forgive them. At the same time, Jews try to learn from their mistakes and resolve to behave better in the coming year. This is the time of repentance which gives the festival its name.

Yom Kippur is celebrated on the tenth and last day of the festival. It begins with a feast, held after sunset on the ninth day. On Yom Kippur, the Day of Atonement, Jews will eat nothing between sunrise and sunset. This is to make amends for their wrongs and to prove their determination not to repeat them. In the synagogue all the lamps are lit – their bright light represents hope for a good year ahead.

Above At Yom Kippur, the Day of Atonement, there are special services held at many synagogues. This historical picture shows such an event in the eighteenth century.

29

Glossary

Atone To make amends or say you are sorry.

Backdrop A length of cloth which is used to provide a background for a display. In theatres, backdrops are often painted with details of scenery.

Equinox The two times of year, in spring and autumn, when the hours of daylight equal the hours of night-time.

Executed Put to death by law.

Guru A wise and powerful teacher. The Sikh religion acknowledges the sayings of ten gurus.

Images A word used to describe religious statues or pictures of gods or goddesses.

Incense A mixture of herbs, spices and perfumed oils which gives off a fragrant smell as it burns. Incense is used in many different religious ceremonies.

Lagoon A shallow lake, especially one situated near, or connected to, the sea or a river.

Lunar A word used to describe anything that is related to the moon.

Pagan Someone who is not a Christian, Jew or Muslim. More recently this word has been used to describe someone who does not have any sort of religious beliefs.

Prosperity Having good fortune, especially great wealth.

Prow The front end of a boat.

Shrine A sacred place where people worship a particular god, goddess, or other object of devotion. A shrine can also be a chest or cabinet, built to hold religious relics.

Stern The rear end of a boat.

Synagogue The name of the Jewish place of worship.

Temperate Zones The areas of the earth's surface between the tropical and polar zones in each hemisphere. It is in these temperate zones that the four seasons of autumn, winter, spring and summer are most different.

Tropical Zones The areas of the earth's surface on either side of the Equator between the Tropic of Cancer and the Tropic of Capricorn. The two tropics mark the furthest points north and south at which the sun is overhead during the summer solstice in each hemisphere.

Waning The apparent weakening of the moon's light between full moon and new moon.

Waxing The increase in brilliance of the moon's light between new moon and full moon.

Books to Read

These books might be of interest to you. You can get them through your local library. Ask the librarian to help you to find them.

Autumn, by R Whitlock (Wayland, 1987)

Buddhist Festivals, by J Snelling (Wayland, 1985)

Festivals and Celebrations, by R Purton (Basil Blackwell, 1983)

Festivals and Customs, by N J Bull (Arnold Wheaton, 1979)

Festivals Around the World, by P Steele (Macmillan, 1983)

Hindu Festivals, by S Mitter, (Wayland, 1985)

India Celebrates, by J W Watson (Garrard, Illinois, 1974)

Jewish Festivals, by R Turner (Wayland, 1985)

Projects for Autumn, by J Jones (Wayland, 1989)

Sikh Festivals, by S S Kapoor (Wayland, 1985)

Picture Acknowledgements

The publishers would like to thank the following for allowing their pictures to be reproduced in this book:

Chapel Studios 13, 18; Das Picture Library 19, 22, 23, 26, 27; Mary Evans Picture Library 29; The Hutchison Library 12, 20, 21, 25; Photri 6, 11, 24; Tony Stone Worldwide 5, 7; Topham Picture Library 9, 10, 16, 17; and Zefa 4, 8, 14, 15, 28. All artwork is by Maggie Downer. Cover J. Allan Cash Ltd.

Index